THIS BOOK BELONGS TO...

Name: callum. F Age: 11

Favourite player: Spence

2021/2022

My Predictions...	Actual...
Forest's final position:	
6th	
Forest's top scorer:	
grabban	
Championship winners:	
fulham	
Championship top scorer:	
mitrovic	
FA Cup winners:	
forest	
EFL Cup winners:	
liverpool	

Contributors: Peter Rogers

A TWOCAN PUBLICATION

ISBN: 978-1-913362-98-0

PICTURE CREDITS: Action Images, Alamy, Press Association, Rex by Shutterstock.

£9

FOREST

CONTENTS

01 ETHAN HORVATH

POSITION: Goalkeeper

DOB: 09/06/1995

COUNTRY: USA

Nottingham Forest's summer signing of American goalkeeper Ethan Horvath has added real competition to the club's goalkeeping options.

Standing at 6ft 3in, 26-year-old Horvath joined the Reds on a free transfer from Club Brugge and agreed a three-year deal at the City Ground. An experienced stopper, he has been capped by the United States on seven occasions and appears all set to challenge Brice Samba for the No1 spot in Chris Hughton's side.

02 DJED SPENCE

POSITION: Defender

DOB: 09/08/2000

COUNTRY: England

Full-back Djed Spence joined The Reds on loan from Middlesbrough on transfer deadline day this summer and will spend the remainder of the season on Trentside.

At 21, Spence has Sky Bet Championship experience having made over 50 appearances for Boro since joining in 2018 having progressed through the ranks at Fulham.

03 TOBIAS FIGUEIREDO

POSITION: Defender

DOB: 02/02/1994

COUNTRY: Portugal

Central defender Tobias Figueiredo joined Nottingham Forest on a permanent basis ahead of the 2018/19 season - he had spent the second half of the previous campaign on loan at the City Ground from parent club Sporting CP.

A consistent performer under the management of Sabri Lamouchi, Figueiredo continued to impress following the appointment of Chris Hughton and made 34 appearances in all competitions last season.

04 JOE WORRALL

POSITION: Defender

DOB: 10/01/1997

COUNTRY: England

Having been ever-present in Forest's 2019/20 campaign, defender Joe Worrall enjoyed an outstanding 2020/21 at the City Ground which ended with him collecting the club's Player of the Season award.

Having progressed though the Forest Academy, Worrall gained great experience with loan spells at Dagenham & Redbridge and Glasgow Rangers earlier in his career before establishing himself as a mainstay in the Forest backline.

SQUAD 2021/22

ALEX MIGHTEN

SIDE-FOOT PASS

The side-foot pass is one of the most accurate passing techniques over shorter distances. The ability to find one of your teammates with a pass, even when under severe pressure, and retain possession of the ball is an essential factor in the way the game is played today.

SOCCER SKILLS

EXERCISE ONE

Set up a 10 x 10m grid. In one corner there are two players and on each of the other three corners there is one player.

Player A starts with the ball. Each player must pass the ball round the square in sequence then follow their pass. A passes to B then runs after his pass and takes up B's starting position. B passes to C and follows his pass to take C's position, and so on. All of the players must control the ball then pass it with the inside of their foot.

Key Factors

1. **Non-kicking foot alongside the ball.**
2. **Pass with the inside of the foot.**
3. **Strike through the middle of the ball.**
4. **Keep your eyes on the ball and your head steady.**

EXERCISE TWO

The set up is the same as exercise one.

In this exercise the players pass the ball in sequence, A through to D, but do not follow their pass, remaining stationary.

As soon as A plays the first pass, E sets off racing around the outside of the starting point. The players must pass the ball as quickly and accurately as possible while under pressure from E, who cannot tackle but is effectively racing the ball round the square.

The same key factors apply in this exercise as in the first, but the players are required to be able to pass the ball accurately while under pressure.

Any team who can retain possession through good accurate passing will always make it very difficult for the opposition. The side-foot pass is one of the most accurate passing techniques.

Legendary England goalkeeper Peter Shilton played over 200 league games for Forest between 1977 and 1982. He enjoyed a trophy-laden career at the City Ground as Forest secured both domestic and European success.

Shilton began his career with Leicester City and made a £325,000 move to Stoke City in November 1974 – that transfer set a then world record fee for a goalkeeper. It was in September 1977 that Shilton was lured to the City Ground by Brian Clough as Forest paid the Potters £250,000 for his services.

Although Shilton was cup tied for the team's League Cup success in 1977/78, he played a vital role in the League title triumph conceding just 18 goals in 37 league games. He also kept goal in both of Forest's European Cup triumphs of 1979 and 1980.

PETER SHILTON

FOREST HEROES

VOICE

Charged with organising the defensive unit in front of him, goalkeeper Shilton would often be heard barking instructions to his teammates. With the whole pitch in his sight it is an important part of the goalkeeper's role to advise teammates of the dangers he can spot.

FEET

Peter Shilton kept goal for Forest long before the back-pass rule was introduced, however he still used his feet to great effect. His kicking could be relied upon to clear danger swiftly up-field and he would often sprint off his line to thwart attackers in a one-on-one situation.

EYES

Always keeping a close eye on the ball, goalkeeper Peter Shilton used his sight to judge the flight of crosses and the speed of shots heading his way. Sight is such a vital part of goalkeeping particularly when quickly assessing whether to come for a ball or leave it for a defender.

HANDS

Blessed with the ability to quickly bring his hands into action to repel the opposition's efforts on goal, Shilton could always be relied upon to pull off saves and use his hands effectively to either gather the ball or push it to safety.

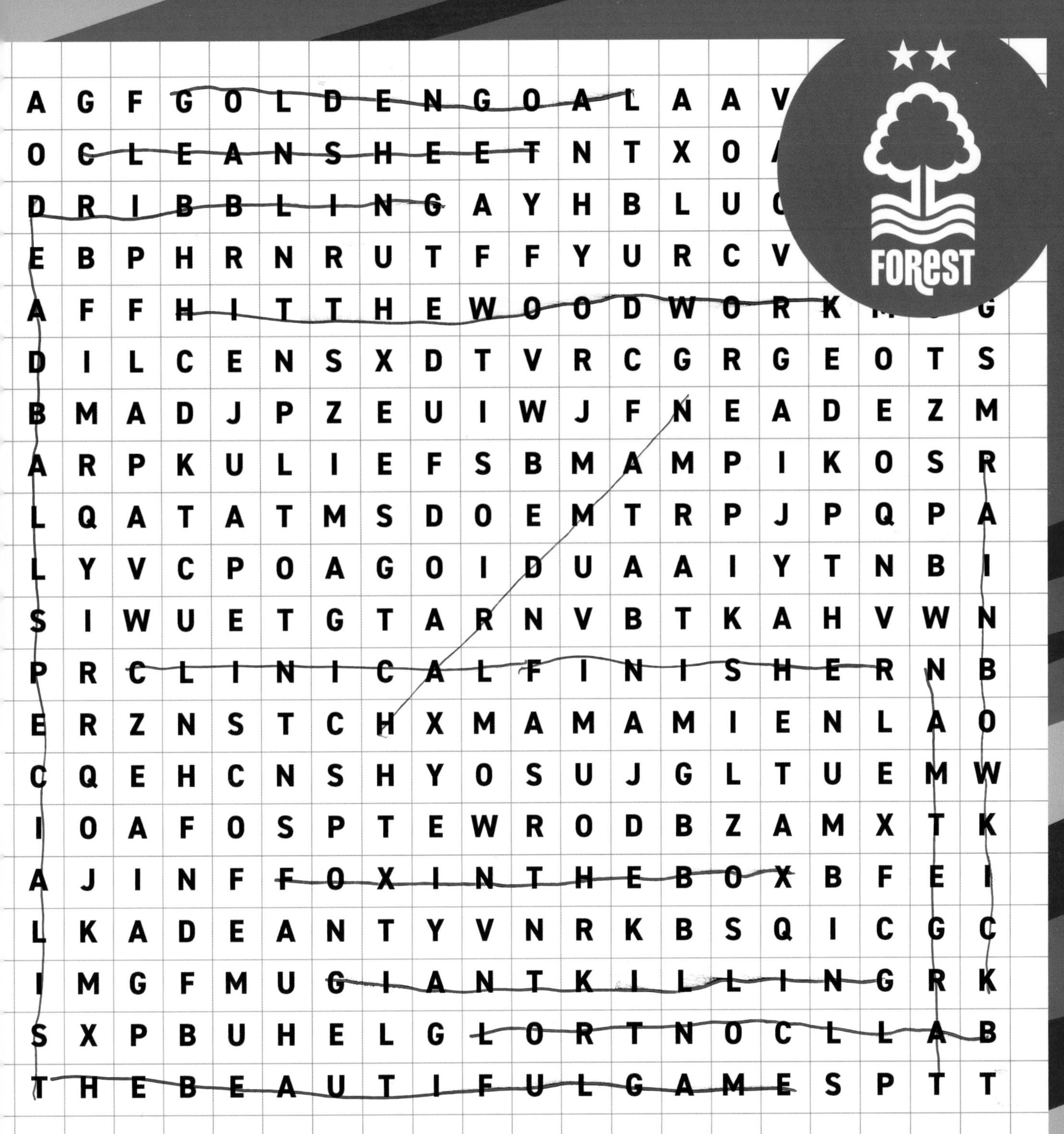

SOCCER SEARCH

ALL OF THESE FOOTY TERMS ARE HIDDEN IN THE GRID, EXCEPT FOR ONE... CAN YOU WORK OUT WHICH ONE?

Ball Control
Bicycle Kick
Boot it
Brace
Clean Sheet

Clinical Finisher
Cruyff Turn
Cup-tied
Dead-ball Specialist
Dribbling

Flip Flap
Fox in the Box
Gaffer
Giant-killing
Golden Goal

Hard Man
Hit the Woodwork
Magic Sponge
Man On
Nutmeg

Rainbow Kick
Skipper
Target Man
The Beautiful Game
Treble

ANSWERS ON PAGE 62

05 RODRIGO ELY

POSITION: Defender

DOB: 03/11/1993

COUNTRY: Brazil

Brazilian defender Rodrigo Ely signed for The Reds following a four-year spell with Spanish side Deportivo Alaves.

The 27-year-old joined AC Milan in 2012 and made four appearances for the Italian giants during his time with the Rossoneri. Rodrigo joins on an initial contract until the end of the 2021/22 campaign.

06 LOIC MBE SOH

POSITION: Defender

DOB: 13/06/2001

COUNTRY: France

Signed from Paris Saint-Germain in September 2020, France youth international Loic Mbe Soh faced a challenging first season in England. The powerful defender made eight first-team appearances in 2020/21 and following an impressive pre-season, he won a place in Chris Hughton's side for the opening game of the 2021/22 campaign at Coventry City.

Aged 20, Soh is a player with great potential who has the flexibility of being able to operate in central defence or at right-back.

07 LEWIS GRABBAN

POSITION: Forward

DOB: 12/01/1988

COUNTRY: England

Striker Lewis Grabban topped the Forest scoring charts again in 2020/21 and his vast Championship experience continues to be a real asset to the Reds' squad.

The 33-year-old Londoner has now made over a century of league appearances for Forest since arriving at the City Ground in the summer of 2018. As the 2021/22 season got underway, Grabban was just seven goals shy of 50 in Forest colours.

SQUAD 2021/22

08 JACK COLBACK

POSITION: Midfielder

DOB: 24/10/1989

COUNTRY: England

An all-action midfielder, Jack Colback has won many admirers with his committed performances in the Reds' engine room.

Having made 55 appearances in a Forest shirt during two loan spells at the City Ground, Colback joined the club on a permanent basis in the summer of 2020 following his release from Newcastle United. An experienced campaigner, Colback began his career with Sunderland and has also played for Ipswich during a loan spell at Portman Road.

Can you find him?

There are five Robin Hoods hiding in the crowd as fans cheer on the lads in 1977.

CLASSIC FANTASTIC

ANSWERS ON PAGE 62

DESIGN A KIT

Have a go at creating next season's home kit for Forest!

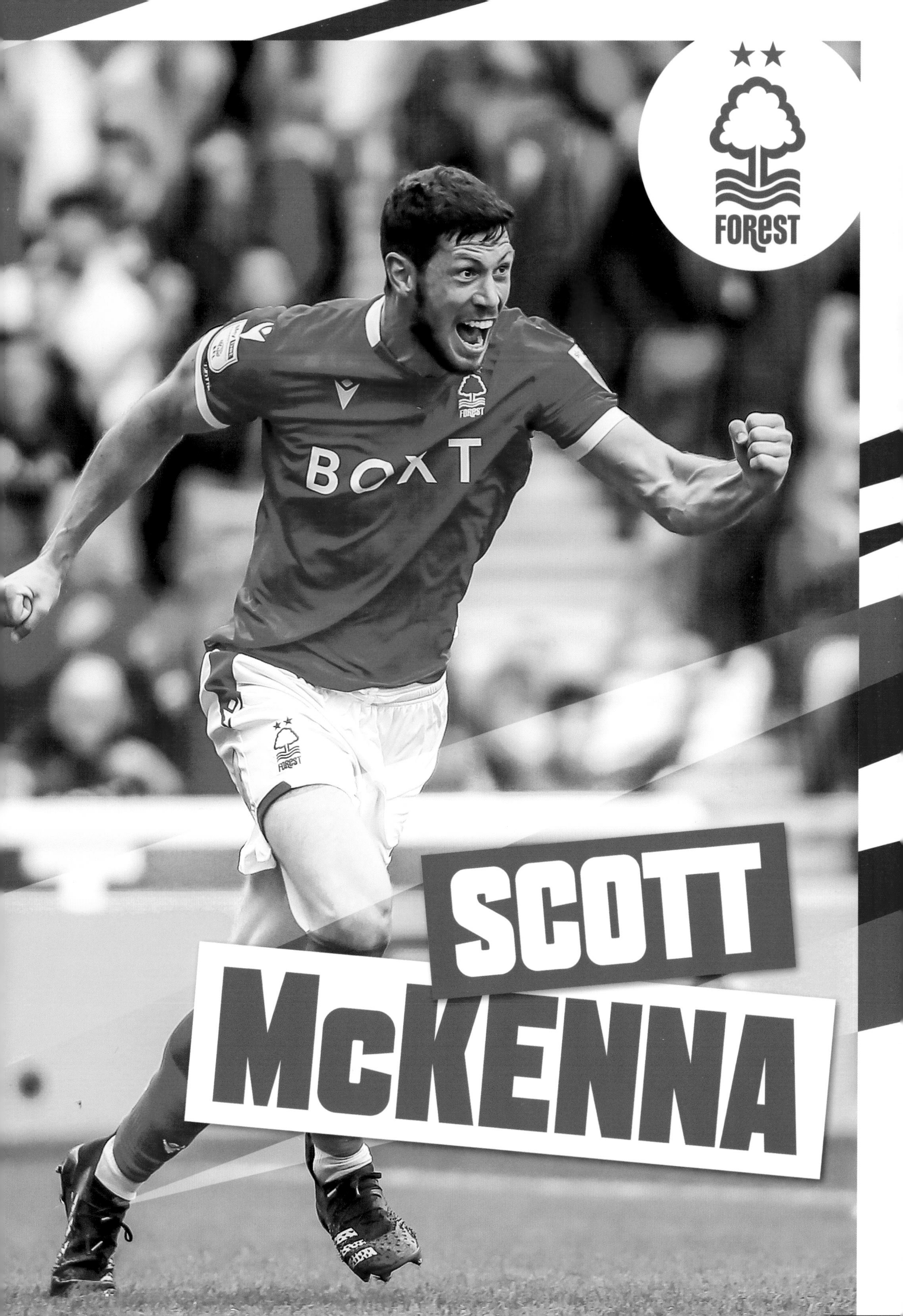
FOREST
BOXT
SCOTT
McKENNA

Nottingham Forest's proud red and white colours have been a long-held tradition at the City Ground. However, a great deal of excitement and anticipation still surrounds the launch of every new Forest kit. Each and every playing strip forms its own part of the Reds' proud history and supporters young and old will all have their own favourites. Let's take a look back at four of the best...

1977/78

Nottingham Forest teamed up with kit manufacturer adidas following the team's promotion back to the top flight in 1977 and a classic Forest kit was produced which coincided with the most successful era in the club's history. This strip was worn over a three-season spell as Forest enjoyed major success both domestically and in Europe.

A traditional red shirt with a white v-neck collar and white cuffs was enhanced with the three adidas stripes in white on the shoulders and arms. The club crest and manufacturer's logo were housed on the chest area. This was of course in a period before shirt sponsorship had become commonplace.

The all-white shorts carried three Adidas stripes in red on the side and the manufacturer's motif on the front. An all-red sock was topped with three white bands in true adidas style.

DRESSED TO IMPRESS

Promoted from the Second Division the previous season, Forest took the First Division by storm in 1977/78.

Under the inspirational management of Brian Clough, Forest stunned the football world by winning the First Division title, finishing a whopping seven points clear of reigning champions Liverpool who ended the season as runners-up. Not only were Forest league champions in 1977/78 but they won the League Cup too after defeating Liverpool in the final.

HE WORE IT WELL

Striker Tony Woodcock fired home vital goals in both league and cup competitions as Forest were crowned First Division Champions and League Cup winners in 1977/78.

Alongside strike-partner Peter Withe, Woodcock ended the season with 19 goals in all competitions - eleven in the First Division, four in the club's triumphant League Cup campaign and a further four in the FA Cup.

Having produced the Forest strip from 1986, Umbro gave Brian Clough's men a smart new .ook for the 1988/89 season.

A classic all-red shirt with a round neck and a trendy button down white collar with red and black trim was introduced for a two-season period from 1988 to 1990. The design saw the black and white theme from the collar also used on the cuffs too. The club crest, manufacturer's motif and sponsor's logo were all displayed on the front of the shirt.

White shorts with a chequered background carried a black and red flash on the side with the club crest and Umbro logo on the front. The socks were all red with the Umbro logo displayed on the shin pad area.

DRESSED TO IMPRESS

t was while wearing this strip that Forest rekindled their affection for League Cup glory. The club had won the trophy in back-to-back seasons in the late '70s and they repeated that feat again by winning the cup in 1988/89 and then retaining the trophy again in 1989/90.

A memorable league campaign saw Brian Clough's side finish third in the First Division, while Wembley glory and the League Cup trophy were secured following a 3-1 victory over current holders Luton Town in the final. The club also won the Full Members Cup at Wembley in 1988/89.

HE WORE IT WELL

For the fourth consecutive season talented striker Nigel Clough topped the goalscoring charts at the City Ground in 1988/89.

The son of manager Brian, Clough Jnr netted 21 goals as Forest enjoyed a Wembley double and a third-place league finish. He was Forest's two-goal hero as the team defeated Luton Town to win the League Cup. Trailing 1-0 at the break, Clough levelled from the penalty spot on 54 minutes before then netting his second and Forest's third goal of the game to wrap up a 3-1 victory 14 minutes from time.

ALL KITTED OUT

SQUAD 2021/22

10 JOAO CARVALHO

POSITION: Midfielder

DOB: 09/03/1997

COUNTRY: Portugal

The 2021/22 season sees talented midfielder Joao Carvalho back at the City Ground having spent the previous season on loan in Spain with UD Almeria.

The Portuguese playmaker first joined the Reds in the summer of 2018 but with first-team opportunities limited under the previous manager he spent the 2020/21 campaign out on loan. Carvalho returned to Forest in the summer and appears to have a fresh lease of life under Chris Hughton with the 24-year-old marking his first appearance of the season with two goals in the League Cup victory over Bradford City.

11 PHILIP ZINCKERNAGEL

POSITION: Forward

DOB: 16/12/1994

COUNTRY: Denmark

Danish winger Philip Zinckernagel joined Nottingham Forest on a season-long loan from Premier League Watford in August 2021.

The winger featured in 20 Championship fixtures as the Hornets secured automatic promotion back to the Premier League last season and the Dane's ability to perform in a number of attacking positions is sure to benefit Chris Hughton's side throughout the 2021/22 campaign.

12 JORDAN SMITH

POSITION: Goalkeeper

DOB: 08/12/1994

COUNTRY: England

A product of the club's Academy, goalkeeper Jordan Smith has now played over half a century of games in the Forest goal.

He made his Reds' debut against Norwich City back in February 2017 and has since taken in loan spells with Barnsley and Mansfield Town. He produced a number of impressive displays in pre-season ahead of the 2021/22 campaign and together with Brice Samba and Ethan Horvath provides real depth to the club's goalkeeping department.

Keeping fit and healthy is vital for all of us. So if you play footy for the school team or your local club, being fit and ready for action is sure to help you enjoy the game and perform to your very best.

For the players at Nottingham Forest, showing peak levels of fitness is essential if they want to feature in Chris Hughton's team. Before anyone can think of pulling on the famous red shirt and taking to the pitch at the City Ground on a Saturday afternoon, they will have had to perform well in training at Wilford Lane and to have shown the manager, his coaches and fitness staff that they are fully fit and ready for the physical challenges that await them on a matchday.

Regardless of whether training takes place at the training ground or at the stadium, the players' fitness remains an all-important factor.

Of course, time spent working on training drills and playing small-sided games will help a player's fitness, but there is lots of work undertaken just to ensure maximum levels of fitness are reached. Away from the training pitches the professional players will spend a great deal of time in the gymnasium partaking in their own personal workouts. Bikes, treadmills and weights will all form part of helping the players reach and maintain a top level of fitness.

Over the course of a week the players will take part in many warm-up and aerobic sessions and even complete yoga and pilates classes to help with core strength and general fitness. The strength and conditioning coaches at the club work tirelessly to do all they can to make sure that the Forest players you see in action on a matchday really are fighting fit for footy!

GET FIT FOR FOOTY

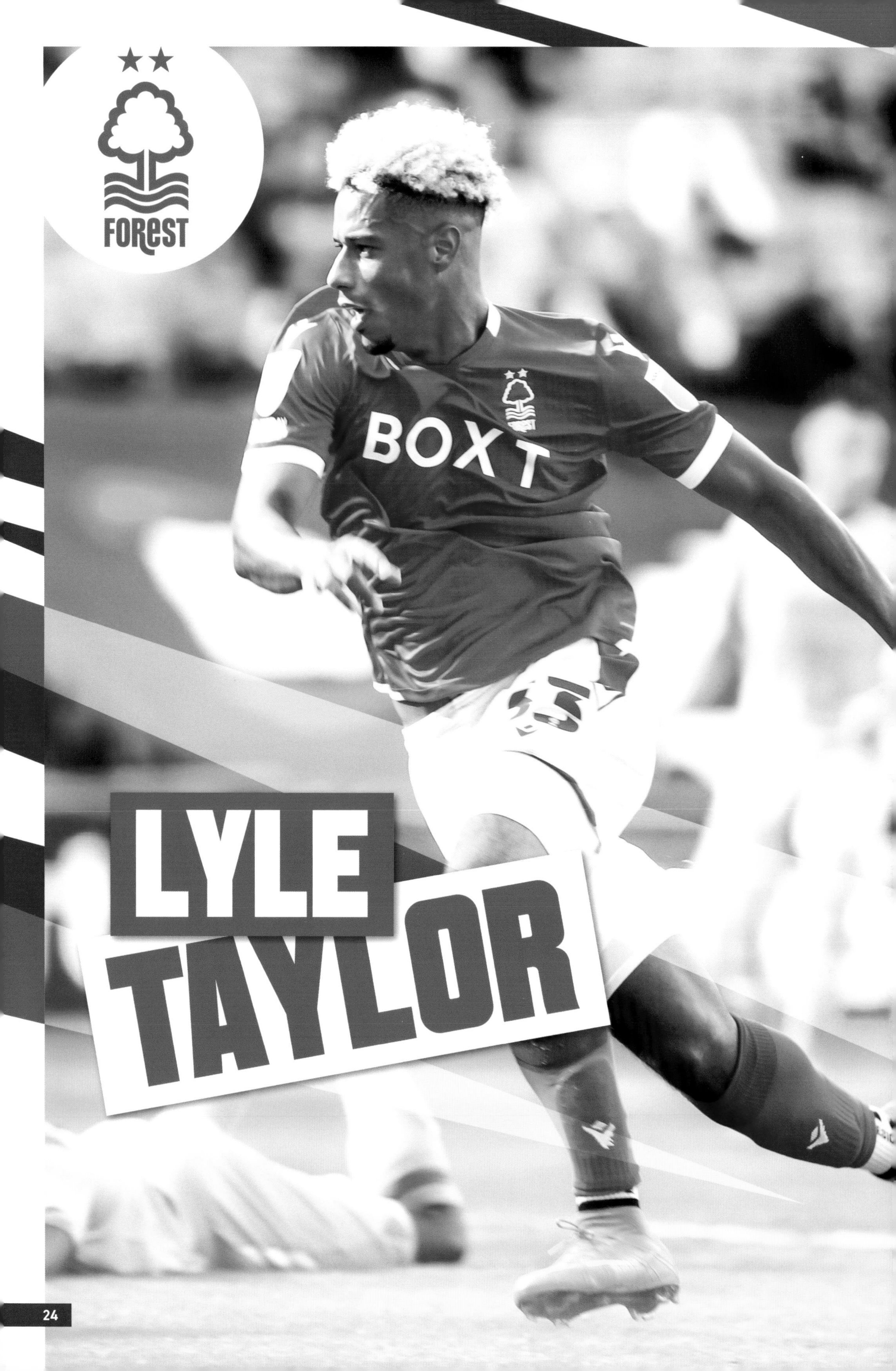
FOREST
BOXT
LYLE
TAYLOR

It has been said that dribbling is a dying art. The pace of the modern game makes it more difficult, but there are players about, even in today's lightning fast conditions, who have the confidence to keep hold of the ball and take on defenders.

DRIBBLING

SOCCER SKILLS

EXERCISE ONE

As a warm-up exercise, players A and B each dribble a ball around a 20 x 10m grid, avoiding each other, but staying within the grid boundary lines.

They progress to a 'cat and mouse' race between the corners - the player with the most visits to each corner wins the race. One of the main problems in this exercise is avoiding the other player, and their ball.

EXERCISE TWO

Now for a more realistic exercise. Six players are used as shown, with three attackers and three defenders at any one time. When play starts, the players with the ball attack any of the three opposing goals, changing their target as they choose. The defenders have, simply, to stop their opposite number from scoring, but must not interfere with any other pair.

Key Factors

1. **Close control.**
2. **Quick change of direction.**
3. **Acceleration away from defender.**
4. **Feints, to wrong-foot defender.**
5. **Head up to see the whole picture.**

When the defenders win possession, they become the attackers, and go for goal themselves. This can be a very enjoyable practice, but also quite tiring.

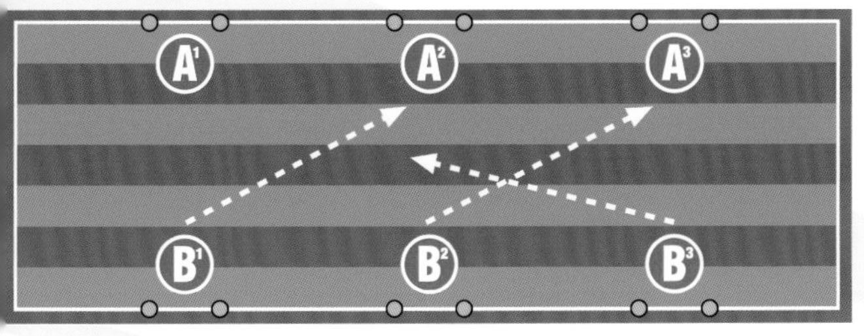

FOREST
1
ANSWER
2
1932
ANSWER
3
ANSWER
4
ANSWER
5
ANSWER

GUESS THE CLUB

6

ANSWER

7

ANSWER

8

ANSWER

Each football holds the clues to the identity of a Premier League or Football League club, how quickly can you solve them?

9

ANSWER

10

ANSWER

ANSWERS ON PAGE 62

13 GAETAN BONG

POSITION: Defender

DOB: 25/04/1988

COUNTRY: Cameroon

A vastly experienced defender, Cameroon international Gaetan Bong joined Nottingham Forest in the 2020 January transfer window.

Bong had been an impressive performer at Brighton & Hove Albion prior to his arrival at the City Ground. Following the appointment of his former Seagulls' boss Chris Hughton as Forest manager, Bong made a dozen appearances in all competitions for Hughton in 2020/21.

15 MAX LOWE

POSITION: Defender

DOB: 11/05/1997

COUNTRY: England

With the 2021/22 Championship campaign underway, Forest swooped for England youth international Max Lowe who joined the club on loan for the remainder of the season from Sheffield United.

The 24-year-old left-back, who can also feature in a more advanced role, began his career at Derby County before joining the Blades in September 2020 and making eight Premier League appearances for the Bramall Lane club last season.

SQUAD 2021/22

17 ALEX MIGHTEN

POSITION: Forward

DOB: 11/04/2002

COUNTRY: England

England youth international winger Alex Mighten added goals to his game last season after initially appearing on the first-team scene in a September 2019 League Cup tie at Arsenal.

An exciting winger, Mighten netted his first career goal to ensure Forest picked up a point from their December 2020 trip to Millwall. He was then on target in the home victories over Blackburn Rovers and Queens Park Rangers. The teenager is expected to play a key role for the Reds in 2021/22.

18 CAFU

POSITION: Midfielder

DOB: 26/02/1993

COUNTRY: Portugal

Carlos Dias, known more commonly as 'Cafu', initially arrived at the City Ground in October 2020 on loan from Olympiacos.

A vastly-experienced player whose career has seen him sample football in many different countries, the 28-year-old former Portuguese youth international was seen as a defender when he joined the club but has been converted to play in a more advanced role by Forest boss Chris Hughton.

19 XANDE SILVA

POSITION: Midfielder

DOB: 16/03/1997

COUNTRY: Portugal

Portuguese forward Xande Silva joined The Reds from Premier League outfit West Ham United during the 2021 summer transfer window.

Silva was born in Porto and has represented his country at youth level. The 24-year-old began his senior career with Vitoria Guimaraes before signing for The Hammers in 2018 where a loan spell followed with Greek side Aris.

Nottingham Forest's 2-0 home victory over Sheffield Wednesday last season certainly came at the perfect time for Chris Hughton's side as it ended a frustrating sequence of seven Championship fixtures without a win.

NOTTINGHAM FOREST 2 SHEFFIELD WEDNESDAY 0

TUESDAY, 15 DECEMBER 2020

Although the ongoing Covid-19 pandemic meant the match was played behind closed doors, the result certainly gave supporters watching from home the perfect pre-Christmas boost. With the visitors arriving at the City Ground for this midweek fixture at the foot of the table, the pressure was really on Hughton's men to return to winning ways.

Forest got off to the best possible start when Yuri Ribeiro's fourth-minute strike gave them the lead and settled the nerves. Had there have been a crowd in attendance, the relief would have swept around the ground as Ribeiro's sweet strike nestled in the back of the Wednesday net.

Despite the two sides going into the game low on confidence an entertaining affair soon began to unfold. Lyle Taylor twice went close to adding to the lead while Wednesday almost worked a first-half equaliser when Adam Reach failed to connect with the ball at the far post.

Forest carried a real threat throughout the second half but their impressive approach play was not rewarded with the second goal that the team craved. As time ticked by with such a slender advantage, there was always the fear that a rare Owls attack could see Forest's advantage wiped out. However, all fears of a tricky ending were extinguished when substitute Lewis Grabban made a welcome return from injury by robbing Wednesday defender Tom Lees of possession and crashing home his first goal of the season to secure all three points with just three minutes left on the clock.

This win was Forest's fourth in 19 Championship outings and moved them three points clear of the relegation zone and seven clear of Wednesday.

After the match boss Hughton confirmed this really had been a vital triumph and one his players were fully deserving of.

"It's a big relief," said the City Ground boss. "It's been tough I must admit and it's been tough on the players as well.

"With regard to endeavour and effort in certain games I can't fault them for that," added Hughton.

GAME OF THE SEASON

STAN COLLYMORE

Striker Stan Collymore displayed sensational goalscoring form over a two-year City Ground career under the management of Frank Clark.

After rising to fame with an impressive goals-to-games ratio during his Southend United career, Collymore joined Forest in the summer of 1993 for a £2M transfer fee. He hit the ground running and his goals helped the team's march up the table as Forest secured automatic promotion and an immediate return to the Premier League.

If his first season at Forest was impressive, then his second was outstanding - Collymore hammered home 22 Premier League goals as Forest finished third in the top flight. His form subsequently led to Liverpool paying a then British record transfer fee of £8.5M for him in the summer of 1995.

FOREST HEROES

HEADERS

Despite being renowned as a player with great pace and power, a number of Stan Collymore's Forest goals came from headers. A real threat in the air, Stan had the power to out-jump defenders and then use his head to direct the ball past the 'keeper and into the net. Once the ball was in and around the six-yard box and in the air there was always a good chance Stan would head it home.

ENCOURAGEMENT

As the focal point of the attack, Collymore could be relied upon to advise and encourage teammates to play the ball into areas where he could be most effective and cause danger to the opposition.

GOALS

More than capable of scoring with his head, the majority of Stan's goals for Forest came from his lethal right foot. With the ability to take shots first time or end a positive forward run with a blistering strike - whenever Stan pulled the trigger with his right foot, it rarely let him down.

CHEST CONTROL

As a strong centre forward who led the Forest attack so well, Stan Collymore was blessed with a great ability to play with his back to goal and take the ball under control on his chest. He could then hold up play while others arrived in support or lay the ball off to a teammate.

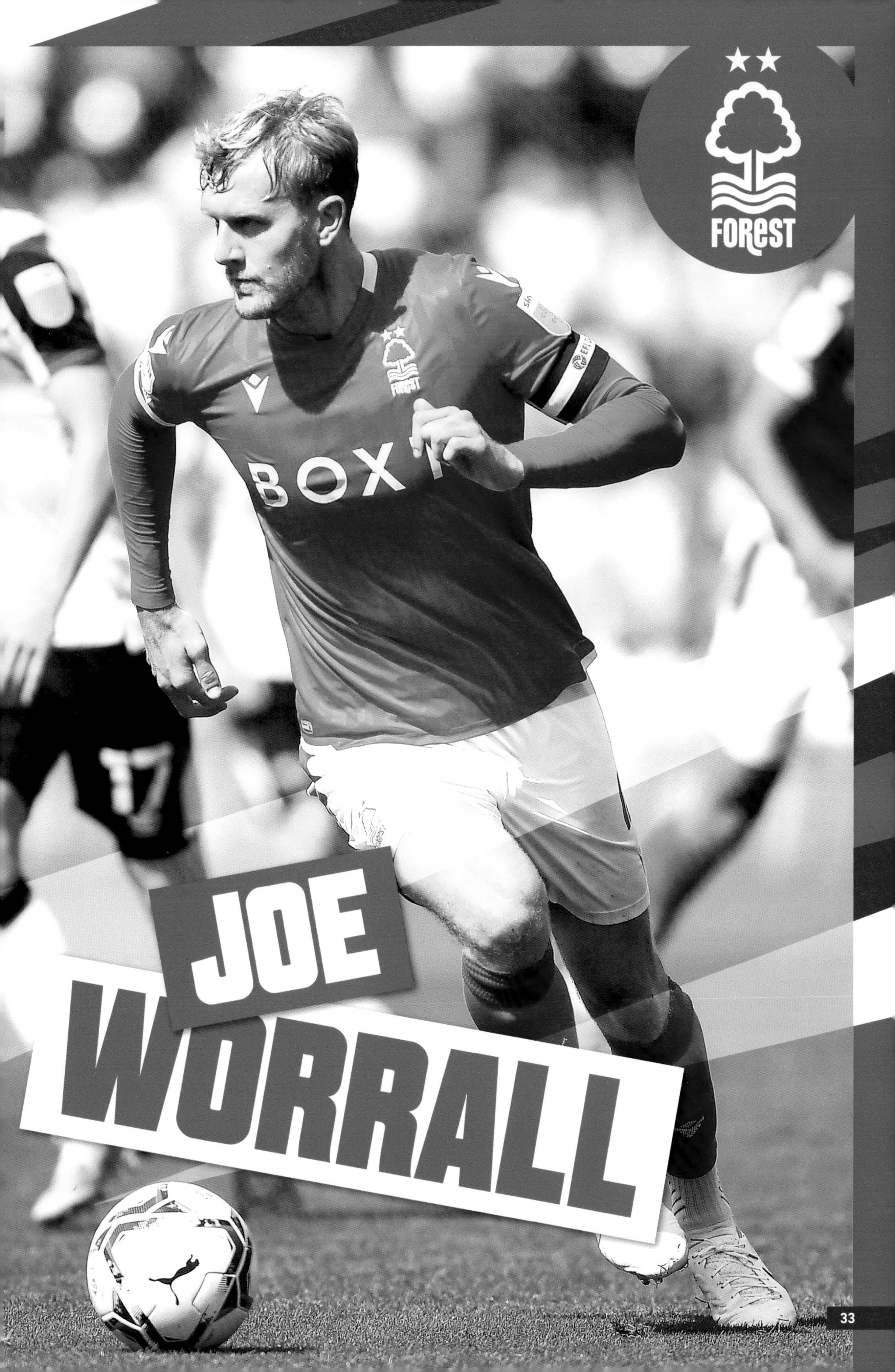
FOREST
BOXT
JOE
WORRALL

RECORD ATTENDANCE

As we all know there are few better places to be than inside a packed City Ground and helping cheer the Reds on to victory. The record attendance for a game at the City Ground was set on 28 October 1967 when 49,946 fans were shoehorned in to witness a Joe Baker brace and a Frank Wignall goal give Forest a 3-0 First Division lead against Manchester United.

Although George Best pulled a goal back for the reigning First Division champions, the hosts held on for a memorable 3-1 victory to send the Forest faithful among the bumper crowd home happy.

TOP SCORER IN A SEASON

The goals of centre forward Wally Ardron proved to be a vital ingredient in Nottingham Forest's 1950/51 Division Three (South) title-winning campaign.

Although Grenville Morris tops the club's overall league scoring charts, Ardron's 36 league goals in 1950/51 remain the best-ever return in a single season from a Forest player.

Ardron joined Forest from Rotherham United in 1949 and proceeded to hammer home an incredible 123 league goals from 182 games for the club in a six-season period from 1949/50 to 1954/55.

YOUNGEST PLAYER

Exciting forward Craig Westcarr took the mantle of becoming Nottingham Forest's youngest-ever player when he debuted against Burnley on 13 October 2001.

The Nottingham-born youngster was aged just 16 years 257 days old when he replaced David Johnson seven minutes from time in a 1-0 victory over the Clarets at the City Ground.

Westcarr made a further 22 league appearances for Forest and took in loan spells at Lincoln City and MK Dons. Following his release from Forest, he spent a period on the non-league scene before returning to the Football League with neighbours Notts County.

RECORD MAKERS

A selection of players, games, facts and figures which all shape the club's proud history.

MOST INTERNATIONAL CAPS

Club legend Stuart Pearce proudly holds the record as Nottingham Forest's most capped international player. An outstanding left-back, Pearce made over 400 league appearances for Forest in a twelve-year career that spanned between 1985 and 1997. He won 76 of his 78 caps for England while plying his trade at the City Ground.

A double League Cup winner with Forest in 1988/89 and again in 1989/90, he was also an FA Cup finalist in 1991. Pearce has since managed the club and also taken charge of the England team at U21 level.

RECORD APPEARANCE MAKER

An accomplished defender and loyal one-club servant, Bob McKinlay made a club record 692 appearances for Nottingham Forest across a 19-season City Ground career.

Between 1959 and 1965, McKinlay was ever present in six consecutive seasons. He was a member of the club's 1959 FA Cup winning side and also a promotion winner back in 1956/57.

He played his final game for the club in November 1969 and subsequently joined the coaching staff at the City Ground. A true Forest legend, his record number of games for the club is unlikely to ever be surpassed.

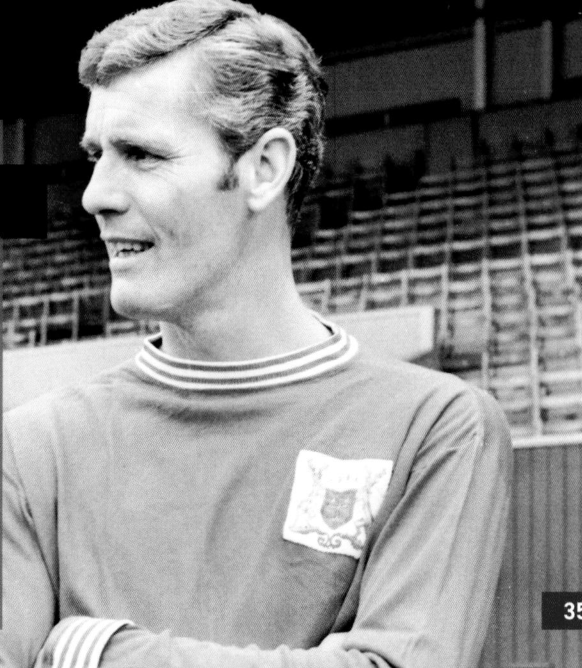

20 BRENNAN JOHNSON

POSITION: Forward

DOB: 23/05/2001

COUNTRY: Wales

After breaking into the Forest first team in the 2019/20 campaign young forward Brennan Johnson gained valuable first team experience with a successful season-long loan at Lincoln City in 2020/21.

He fired home 13 goals for the Imps who reached the League One Play-Off final. After returning to the City Ground in the summer he instantly impressed boss Chris Hughton and the Forest coaching staff to win a place in the starting line-up at the beginning of the season.

SQUAD 2021/22

21 BRAIAN OJEDA

POSITION: Midfielder

DOB: 27/06/2000

COUNTRY: Paraguay

Paraguayan international midfielder Braian Ojeda was another summer recruit having joined from Olimpia.

The 21-year-old has represented the Paraguay national team since U17 level and made his senior debut in the 2022 World Cup qualifying campaign in September.

22 RYAN YATES

POSITION: Midfielder

DOB: 21/11/1997

COUNTRY: England

Tough-tackling midfielder Ryan Yates firmly established himself as a regular face in the Forest first team in 2020/21. Having progressed through the Forest Academy set-up, Lincoln-born Yates made 28 appearances last season and chipped in with two goals in the opening months of 2021.

He netted the Reds' third goal in the 3-1 home victory over Millwall in January and then scored the only goal of the game to ensure Forest picked up all three points from their February trip to Rotherham.

23 JOE LOLLEY

POSITION: Forward

DOB: 25/08/1992

COUNTRY: England

Signed from Huddersfield Town in January 2018, Joe Lolley brings both Championship and Premier League experience to the Forest squad.

A real creative spark in the Reds' frontline and an undoubted match winner, Lolley was in the right place at the right time to score a last-minute winner away to Blackburn Rovers in October 2020 to ensure new manager Chris Hughton got off to the perfect start as Forest boss.

IMPOSSIBLE Footy Decisions

Would you rather...

have to play the rest of your football games in 35 degree heat or a blizzard?

Would you rather...

have Lyle Taylor's ability to score goals or Brice Samba's ability to save them?

Would you rather...

have a pause button or a rewind button for your life?

Would you rather...

have unlimited battery life on all your devices or free wifi wherever you go?

Would you rather...

run 100 laps of the pitch or complete 200 burpees?

Would you rather...

score the FA Cup final winning goal against the Rams in your only game for Nottingham Forest or play 300 games for Forest in League One?

Would you rather...

be remembered for a terrible footy howler or be forgotten completely?

Would you rather...

sell your best player to Derby County for £50m or sell him abroad for £20m?

Would you rather...

have to take a penalty against Brice Samba or have Joao Carvalho take a penalty against you?

Would you rather...

sit right at the back during a game or have the best seats in the stadium, but not be allowed to eat, drink or use the bathroom?

Would you rather...

be the star in League Two or a squad player in the Premier League?

Would you rather...

Forest win the FA Cup or England win the World Cup?

Would you rather...

your match superstition be wearing the same socks for a season or the same underwear for a month?

Would you rather...

lose on television or win with nobody watching?

Would you rather...

have a long, average playing career or have a short, fantastic career cut short by injury?

Would you rather...

lose to Derby County twice and finish top or beat them twice and finish bottom?

Would you rather...

clean the dressing room toilet with your toothbrush or the floor with your tongue?

Would you rather...

play only five minutes for Forest or win the Premier League with the Rams?

Would you rather...

have to wear every shirt inside out or every pair of pants backwards?

Would you rather...

give up your mobile phone for a month or bathing for a month?

Would you rather...

be alone all your life or surrounded by Derby County supporters?

Would you rather...

play for Forest and always lose or sit on the bench and Forest always win?

Would you rather...

the half-time menu got rid of pies or pop?

Would you rather...

become a legendary manager or a legendary player?

JACK COLBACK

A real fans' favourite at the City Ground, Stuart Pearce played a staggering 524 games for Forest and hammered home an incredible 89 goals from the left-back berth during an unforgettable 12-year spell with the club.

A robust and fully-committed defender, Pearce's determination saw him idolised by the City Ground faithful who almost viewed him as a supporter on the pitch such was his commitment to the club. An inspirational leader, Pearce spent the majority of his City Ground career as captain.

Part of an excellent Forest team in the late 80s and early 90s, Pearce and his teammates reached a hat-trick of consecutive League Cup finals at Wembley. Forest were League Cup winners in 1989 after defeating Luton Town 3-1. They regained the trophy the following season with a narrow 1-0 success over Oldham Athletic but suffered a 1-0 defeat to Manchester United in 1991.

STUART PEARCE

FOREST HEROES

TEMPERAMENT

Often faced with containing tricky wingers, Stuart Pearce had the perfect mindset for defending. He very rarely lost concentration and always kept his cool. In the heat of any on-field duel, Pearce kept his mind on the task in hand and more often than not came out on top in one-on-one situations.

QUICK ON HIS HEELS

Stuart Pearce was always alive and alert to danger and when it occurred he was quick on his heels to track and tackle opponents. Not only was he swift over the ground but he was also quick to leap and win headed duels too.

RALLYING CALL

Handed the captain's armband by Brian Clough, Pearce's ability to lead and inspire his teammates was there for all to see. Always there with an encouraging call to those around him, Pearce led by example and was never afraid to let players know if standards had dropped.

LEFT FOOT HAMMER

Always comfortable with the ball at his feet, Pearce was an accomplished ball-playing full-back who could always be relied upon to bring the ball out of defence and help the side turn defence to attack. His trusty left foot was also a great weapon at set piece situations as he hammered home penalties and free-kicks galore.

1994/95

Forest's 1994/95 kit took on something of a radical new look as a great deal of black was introduced to the traditional red and white offering.

The red shirt had a black v-neck collar with a thin white trim while a large black panel was added to the side of the shirt that linked up the shoulder and sleeve areas. The sponsor's branding sat in the centre of the shirt with white piping above and below. The club crest, on a white shield, plus the manufacturer's logo were then housed on the chest area.

A predominately white pair of shorts carried the club crest and Umbro logo while being decorated with a red trim and black piping along the bottom with a black panel on each side. The all-red socks were topped with a black band with white trim and the Umbro motif.

DRESSED TO IMPRESS

Having secured promotion back to the Premier League at the first attempt in 1993/94, Nottingham Forest proved to be the surprise package of the 1994/95 season.

Now under the management of former City Ground favourite Frank Clark, Forest made a flying start to life back among the big boys as they won eight of their opening eleven league games and remained unbeaten until late October. They ended a memorable campaign with a third-place finish and secured the return of European football to the City Ground for the following campaign.

HE WORE IT WELL

One of the first names on manager Frank Clark's team sheet during the 1994/95 season was all-action midfielder Steve Stone.

An energetic player, Stone operated on the right side and missed just one league game in 1994/95 while chipping in with five goals too. His impressive performances over the course of the season at club level were rewarded with an international debut for England in October 1995.

Forest's all-red home shirt which was worn from 2006 to 2008 had some attractive small white flashes on the shoulders, side panels and at the base of the shirt, while also having a neat white round-neck. Manufactured by Umbro, the shirt carried the club crest, sponsor's branding and Umbro motif on the front in the traditional locations.

The brilliant white shorts were decorated with small red flashes on the sides, at the top and bottom, to marry up with the design of the shirts. The manufacturer's logo and club crest were also displayed on the front of the shorts.

An all-red sock carried white flashing at the top with the Umbro branding sitting on the front in the shin pad area.

DRESSED TO IMPRESS

Nottingham Forest ended a three-season spell in the third tier of English football as manager Colin Calderwood guided the club to promotion as League One runners-up in 2007/08.

The team put their Play-Off disappointment of the previous season behind them to secure promotion alongside Swansea City and Doncaster Rovers. Calderwood's men amassed 82 points with top scorer Junior Agogo and Kris Commons among the side's star performers.

HE WORE IT WELL

Any successful season is built upon a solid defence and in 2007/08 Forest certainly had the best final line of defence in the shape of ever-present goalkeeper Paul Smith.

Smith ended the season with 24 clean sheets from his 46 League One outings, the best in the division that season. His heroics in the Forest goal in 2007/08 saw him rewarded with the Puma Golden Glove award for League One.

ALL KITTED OUT

24 JORDI OSEI-TUTU

POSITION: Defender

DOB: 02/10/1998

COUNTRY: England

Young Arsenal defender Jordi Osei-Tutu agreed a season-long loan at the City Ground in August 2021 and will add both cover and competition for the full-back positions.

Having progressed though the Gunners' Academy, Osei-Tutu enhanced his footballing education with a loan spell at German Second Division side VfL Bochum in 2019/20. Upon his return to the UK, he spent last season at Cardiff City where he made nine first-team appearances during a season-long loan in South Wales.

25 MOHAMED DRAGER

POSITION: Defender

DOB: 25/06/1996

COUNTRY: Tunisia

Born in Germany, Mohamed Drager is a Tunisian international and signed for The Reds on a permanent transfer from Olympiacos this summer.

Having risen through the ranks at German outfit Freiburg, Drager spent time on loan with Paderborn between 2018 and 2020 before joining the Greek champions. Drager's addition will add strong competition for places among The Reds' back-line.

SQUAD 2021/22

POSITION: Defender

DOB: 12/11/1996

COUNTRY: Scotland

Scotland international defender Scott McKenna joined Nottingham Forest from Aberdeen in September 2020 and agreed a four-year deal with the Reds.

McKenna arrived at the City Ground with a glowing reputation for both his defensive and leadership qualities - two facets of his game that have certainly impressed the Forest faithful. He made 24 Championship appearances for the Reds last season and the Forest defence always looks a tough nut to crack with McKenna forming part of it.

POSITION: Goalkeeper

DOB: 25/04/1994

COUNTRY: France

Having joined Forest in the summer of 2019 goalkeeper Brice Samba has firmly established himself as the club's first-choice stopper over the past two seasons.

Once again handed the goalkeeper's jersey by Chris Hughton for the Reds' opening game of the 2021/22 season at Coventry, Samba is clearly the man that Jordan Smith and Ethan Horvath will need to edge past in pursuit of first-team football. A consistent and impressive performer, Samba is now closing in on a century of games for the club.

FOREST

JOE
LOLLEY

TACKLING

One of a player's greatest assets is the ability to win the ball. The following exercise can be used to improve a player's tackling abilities.

SOCCER SKILLS

EXERCISE

Set up a 10m x 20m grid.

In this two-on-two exercise, the aim of the game is to score a goal by taking the ball past the two opposing defenders, to the end line, and stand on the ball. The defenders just have to stop them.

As well as producing plenty of opportunities for the defenders to tackle, this session will test the defenders' abilities to work together, and communicate.

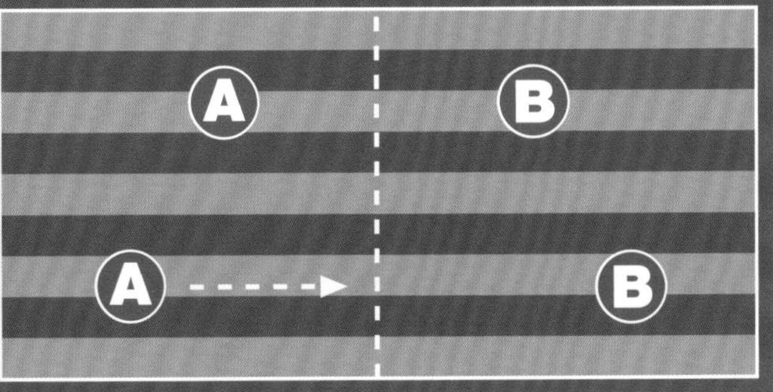

Key Factors

1. **Be patient - do not dive in.**
2. **Stay on your feet if possible.**
3. **Time the tackle with bodyweight behind it.**
4. **Be determined to win it.**

The reason that great players win so many tackles is not just because they know how to tackle and have good technique, it is because they have big hearts and are determined to win their challenges on the pitch.

ODDBALLS

Three of the four pictures in each football represent a Premier League or Football League club, can you figure out the football club as well as the odd one out?

ANSWERS ON PAGE 62

6
A
B
C
D
1905
ANSWER
FOREST
7
A
B
C
D
ANSWER
8
A
B
C
D
ANSWER
9
A
B
C
D
FOOTBALL CLUB
ANSWER
10
A
B
C
D
ANSWER

PLAYER OF THE SEASON

JOE WORRALL

Following the conclusion of the club's 2020/21 Sky Bet Championship campaign, Reds' defender Joe Worrall was named Nottingham Forest's Player of the Year. The 24-year-old was viewed as the team's top performer following a vote by members of the Nottingham Forest Supporters' Club.

A consistent performer in the back four, Worrall made 33 appearances in all competitions for Forest in what was a challenging season at the City Ground. Despite the ongoing Covid-19 pandemic resulting in matches being played behind closed doors and the side adjusting to an early-season change of manager, Worrall remained a tower of defensive strength and was humbled to see his contribution recognised in the end-of-season supporters' poll.

"Growing up watching Forest and being able to play for the club is a dream come true so to be recognised on a personal level means a lot," he said.

"I've been unlucky with the two injuries but coming back into the side and being captain on numerous occasions has been an honour and I've always played each game as though it's my last."

Having progressed through the club's Academy set-up, Hucknell-born Worrall has won international recognition with England at both U20 and U21 level. He gained valuable first-team experience with loan spells at Dagenham & Redbridge and Glasgow Rangers earlier in his career and the defender is now closing in on 150 appearances for Forest.

Worrall appears all set to be one of the first names on manager Chris Hughton's team sheet once the 2021/22 campaign gets underway and the defender will no doubt be looking to enhance his growing reputation even further over the coming months.

YOUNG PLAYER OF THE SEASON

ALEX MIGHTEN

Teenage England forward Alex Mighten claimed the David Howard trophy as Forest's Young Player of the Year for 2020/21.

Mighten made 27 appearances for Forest in all competitions last season and netted three goals, his first securing a valuable point away to Millwall in December 2020. He was also on target in home wins over Blackburn Rovers and Queens Park Rangers

"It's a huge honour to be voted for this award. From coming through the Academy to getting to the point I'm at now - it's been a really enjoyable season on a personal level," he said.

"I've been really grateful to have the chance to play more minutes and gain confidence as a player."

PHILIP ZINCKERNAGEL

BOXT
COLOUR
TOBIAS
FIGUEIREDO

33 LYLE TAYLOR

POSITION: Forward

DOB: 29/03/1990

COUNTRY: Montserrat

A summer 2020 arrival from Charlton Athletic, much-travelled forward Lyle Taylor netted five goals in his first season at the City Ground.

Following an impressive spell with the Addicks, Taylor wasted little time in winning over the Forest faithful as his first goal came against bitter rivals Derby County in the East Midlands derby match. The Montserrat international took the mantle of scoring the club's first goal of the 2021/22 campaign when he netted on the opening weekend against Coventry City.

37 JAMES GARNER

POSITION: Midfielder

DOB: 13/03/2001

COUNTRY: England

Having impressed at the City Ground in the second half of last season, Nottingham Forest were thrilled to secure the services of Manchester United midfielder James Garner on loan again for the 2021/22 campaign.

Garner, who netted four goals in 20 Championship outings for the Reds in 2020/21, was thrust straight back into first-team action upon his return to the City Ground. He made his second Forest debut in the EFL Cup tie with Wolverhampton Wanderers and then started the East Midlands derby match at Pride Park four days later.

SQUAD 2021/22

38 TYRESE FORNAH

POSITION: Midfielder

DOB: 11/09/1999

COUNTRY: England

Tyrese joined the Nottingham Forest Academy in 2019 following a youth spell at Brighton & Hove Albion and is highly regarded on Trentside.

The 21-year-old spent the 2020/21 campaign on loan with Sky Bet League Two side Plymouth Argyle before making his first senior start for The Reds in the Carabao Cup victory against Bradford City in August.

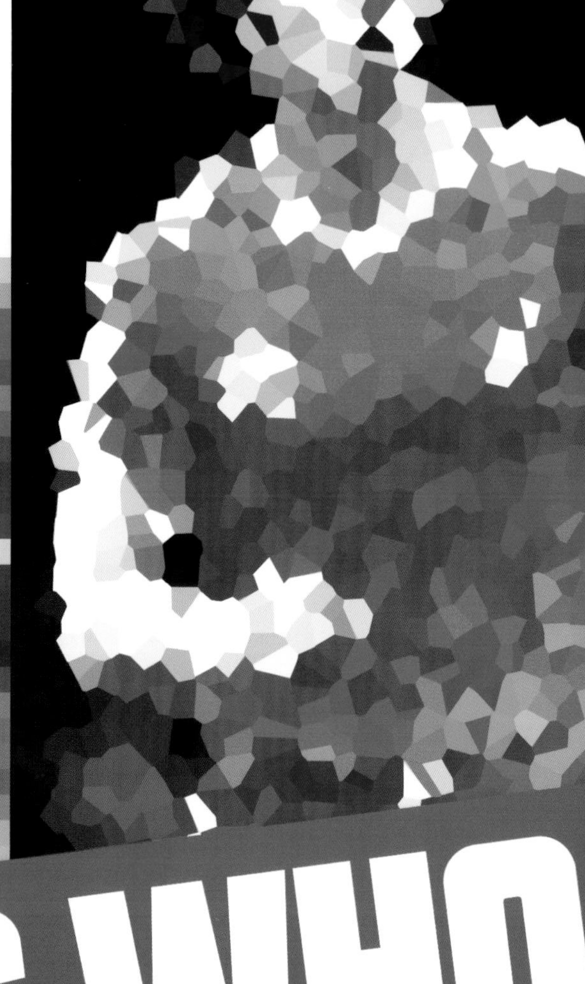

1. WHO AM I?

I was born in Waterford, Ireland in 1983

I rose to prominence in an impressive spell with Ipswich Town

I joined Forest from Newcastle United in the summer of 2017

My first goal in Forest colours came in a 4-3 win at Brentford

I made 32 appearances for the Republic of Ireland and scored three goals as an international

GUESS WHO

2. WHO AM I?

I was born in London but began my career at Forest

I played 346 games for the club and was renowned for my speed

I was capped by England as a Forest player

I was twice a League Cup winner while at the City Ground

After leaving Forest I tried my luck in Italy

3. WHO AM I?

I was born in Plymouth in 1954

I began my career with Birmingham City

I made major headlines when I joined Forest for a record fee

I netted an extremely important goal for the club in May 1979

After leaving the City Ground I joined Manchester City in 1981

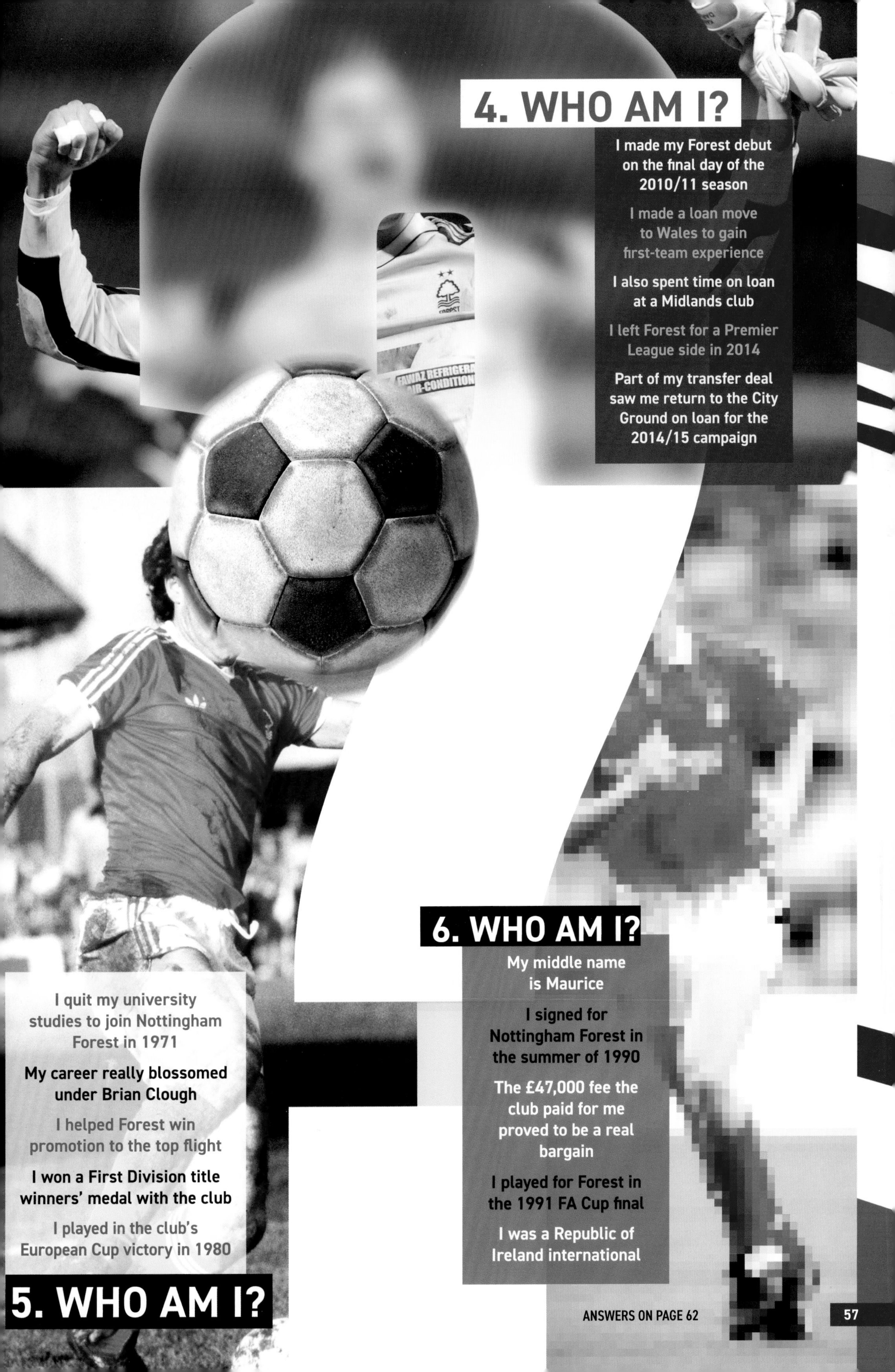

4. WHO AM I?

I made my Forest debut on the final day of the 2010/11 season

I made a loan move to Wales to gain first-team experience

I also spent time on loan at a Midlands club

I left Forest for a Premier League side in 2014

Part of my transfer deal saw me return to the City Ground on loan for the 2014/15 campaign

5. WHO AM I?

I quit my university studies to join Nottingham Forest in 1971

My career really blossomed under Brian Clough

I helped Forest win promotion to the top flight

I won a First Division title winners' medal with the club

I played in the club's European Cup victory in 1980

6. WHO AM I?

My middle name is Maurice

I signed for Nottingham Forest in the summer of 1990

The £47,000 fee the club paid for me proved to be a real bargain

I played for Forest in the 1991 FA Cup final

I was a Republic of Ireland international

ANSWERS ON PAGE 62

JOHN ROBERTSON

Widely regarded as the finest Nottingham Forest player of all time, Scottish international midfielder John Robertson was a star performer in Brian Clough's formidable side that were twice crowned European champions.

The skilful left-winger's ability to run with the ball and cross with the most incredible accuracy saw him play an amazing 243 consecutive games in a four-year spell between December 1976 and December 1980.

After Forest became First Division champions in 1977/78, Robertson starred in both of Forest's European Cup triumphs of 1979 and 1980. He provided the cross for Trevor Francis' winning goal in the 1-0 win over Malmo in 1979 and then proceeded to be the hero of the hour himself when he scored the only goal of the game in the 1980 final against Hamburg.

FOREST HEROES

INTELLIGENCE

A player's football intelligence is often spoken about and John Robertson had it in abundance. He had the skill of making time on the ball, orchestrating the pattern of play and playing creative forward balls. He also had that ability of knowing the runs a teammate would make and the ability to find them with the minimum of fuss.

EYE FOR AN OPENING

Not only was John extremely comfortable on the ball but he also showed great vision and awareness on the pitch. He appeared to have the perfect eye for a quick pass to help Forest mount another attack.

QUICK FEET

Naturally blessed with exceptional close control and dribbling skills, John Robertson had the ability to jinx his way past opponents and into dangerous areas. Always identified as the dangerman, Robertson proved to be a tricky player for opposition to get to grips with.

ADVICE

In his latter years at the City Ground, Robertson used his experience and knowledge gained from playing at the top level for club and country to help the younger players in the Forest team. That era signalled the start of his excellent coaching career.

BRENNAN JOHNSON

FAST FORWARD

Do your predictions for 2021/22 match our own?...

CHAMPIONSHIP WINNERS

Nottingham Forest

CHAMPIONSHIP TOP SCORER

Lewis Grabban

CHAMPIONSHIP RUNNERS-UP

Fulham

CHAMPIONSHIP PLAY-OFF WINNERS

Reading

FA CUP WINNERS

Brighton & Hove Albion

FA CUP RUNNERS-UP

Leeds United

LEAGUE CUP WINNERS

Arsenal

LEAGUE CUP RUNNERS-UP

Watford

PREMIER LEAGUE WINNERS

Manchester United

PREMIER LEAGUE RUNNERS-UP

Chelsea

PREMIER LEAGUE TOP SCORER

Anthony Martial

FOREST TOP APPEARANCE MAKER

Brice Samba

FOREST PLAYER OF THE YEAR

Brennan Johnson

CHAMPIONS LEAGUE WINNERS

Barcelona

CHAMPIONS LEAGUE RUNNERS-UP

Real Madrid

EUROPA LEAGUE WINNERS

West Ham United

EUROPA LEAGUE RUNNERS-UP

Lazio

ANSWERS

PAGE 11
SOCCER SEARCH

Bicycle Kick.

PAGE 14
CLASSIC FANTASTIC

PAGE 26
GUESS THE CLUB

1. Newcastle United. 2. Wigan Athletic. 3. Leeds United. 4. Charlton Athletic. 5. Coventry City. 6. AFC Wimbledon. 7. Stoke City. 8. Millwall. 9.Wolverhampton Wanderers. 10. Burnley.

PAGE 48
ODD BALLS

1. Sunderland, C. 2. Portsmouth, C. 3. Arsenal, B. 4. Crewe Alexandra, A. 5. Queens Park Rangers, C. 6. Crystal Palace, B. 7. Blackburn Rovers, B. 8. Reading, B. 9. Birmingham City, C. 10. West Ham United, D.

PAGE 56
GUESS WHO?

1. Daryl Murphy. 2. Des Walker. 3. Trevor Francis. 4. Karl Darlow. 5. Martin O'Neill. 6. Roy Keane.